D1552670

DUCKS
at play

DUCKS
at play

Sophie Bevan

photography by Alan Williams

RYLAND
PETERS
& SMALL
LONDON NEW YORK

DESIGNER Pamela Daniels
EDITOR Sharon Cochrane
LOCATION RESEARCHER Emily Westlake
PRODUCTION Gavin Bradshaw
ART DIRECTOR Gabriella Le Grazie
PUBLISHING DIRECTOR Alison Starling

First published in the United States
in 2005
by Ryland Peters & Small, Inc.
519 Broadway, 5th Floor
New York, NY 10012
www.rylandpeters.com

10 9 8 7 6 5 4 3 2 1

Text, design, and photographs
© Ryland Peters & Small 2005

ISBN 1 84172 855 1

Printed in China

contents

not-so-ugly duckling

After sitting on her clutch of eggs for about one month, a mother duck is rewarded with a bundle of adorable ducklings. The drake's role can range from doting father figure to fickle philanderer, but it isn't so unusual to see both proud parents showing off their young.

At length one shell cracked, and then another, and from each egg came a living creature that lifted its head and cried, "Peep! Peep!"

HANS CHRISTIAN ANDERSEN,
THE UGLY DUCKLING, 1843

When brand-new ducklings enter the world, they will
bond with the first moving thing they see. Hopefully, this
will be their mother, but it has been known for ducklings
to believe they are human and to follow their owners
around, mimicking their behavior. It has even been known
for an old piece of rusty farmyard machinery to become
the object of a young duckling's affections!

You know that the beginning is the most important part of any work, especially in the case of a young and tender thing.

PLATO (C. 427–347BC)

While it is unclear when man first domesticated the duck, his fascination with these adorable feathered fowl is nothing new. A carved figurine of a flying duck made from the bone of a mammoth was discovered in a German cave and is estimated to be 30,000 years old. This is one of the oldest artworks ever found, making these cavemen the first home owners to decorate their walls with flying ducks.

Founding Feathers

Before the arrival of European settlers, North America was a paradise sanctuary for ducks. When early pioneers arrived on the east coast, they discovered what one British captain described as a "world of fowl." Chesapeake Bay was an area particularly favored by our feathered friends. A seventeenth-century Marylander described seeing a single flight of ducks at the bay that he estimated to be a mile wide and seven miles long! That's quite a lot of duck.

quack quack

Ducks are very sociable creatures. They like
nothing better than to quack about the
barnyard or to splash in the pond with their
siblings, cousins, and companions.
In fact, a duck will befriend just about
anyone—even the family dog.

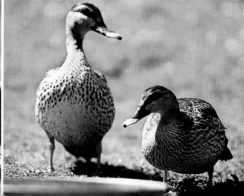

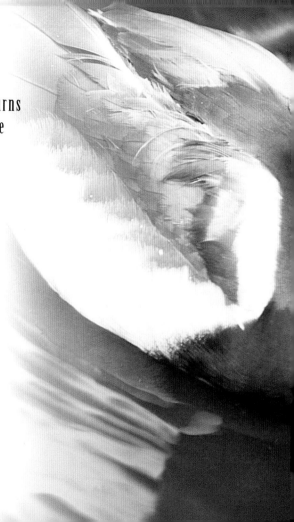

Don't turn in your toes;
a well-brought-up duck turns
its toes quite out, just like
father and mother—so!

HANS CHRISTIAN ANDERSEN,
THE UGLY DUCKLING, 1843

Being gregarious creatures, it's
important that ducks get off
on the right webbed foot with
their companions. But duck chit-
chat is not as straightforward
as you might think. Luckily, the
duck's quack has been the
subject of much rigorous
research from the world's
finest scientific minds …

here a quack ...

Researchers in the U.K. have found that not all quacks are
alike—ducks have regional accents. The Cockney ducks of
east London have a harsh, loud quack, like a shout, reflecting
their gritty urban lives, where they need to be heard over
a lot of noise. Meanwhile, the Cornish country duck has a
laidback, singsong quack, which sounds more like a giggle!

... there a quack ...

The next challenge for the boffins: an old-wives' tale, which claims that a duck's quack is the only noise in the world that has no echo. Volunteer duck Daisy blew the myth out of the water by performing her loudest quack, which echoed across a special sound studio designed to recreate the acoustics of a vast cathedral.

... everywhere
a quack quack

To further muddy the waters of the duck pond, while English-speaking ducks "quack," their foreign cousins have a whole different language. In Bengal, ducks say "gack-gack;" in Hungary, they "háp-háp;" in Albania, it's "mak mak;" and Japanese ducks go "gaa gaa." Luckily, it's only humans that get confused—ducks migrate thousands of miles and never need to take a dictionary!

One world expert in the language of duck was Clarence "Ducky" Nash—the voice of Donald Duck for over five decades. When the Walt Disney cartoon was translated into a foreign language, the script of quacks would be written out phonetically for Clarence to read, and so he learned to quack in a number of languages, including French, Portuguese, Japanese, Chinese, and German.

preening poultry

There's much more to being a duck than simply splashing about in ponds. There's the important business of preening, posturing, trying to walk without a waddle (not easy when you have webbed feet), and generally shaking your tail feathers.

play ducks and drakes

In general, the drake is blessed with the finer plumage. But the female's dull-colored feathers are far more practical because she needs to avoid the attention of any unwanted visitors to her nest. While she's busy protecting her young, she may be disappointed by the new appearance of her handsome, carefully selected partner—once he's secured his mate, he will shed his colorful feathers and look much like the female.

As the wild duck is more swift and beautiful than the tame, so is the wild—mallard—thought, which 'mid falling dews wings its way above the fens.

HENRY DAVID THOREAU,
WALKING, 1862

Ducks often form long-lasting pair bonds, so finding the
right mate is very important. A drake will try all the tricks
in the book to impress the object of his desire, as he struts
around the bathing pool like a bronzed Adonis soaking
up the tropical sun. These include preening, whistling,
flicking his head back, and showing off his many skills in
the air and water.

very important poultry

Of course, not all ducks are created equal. At the Peabody Hotel in Memphis, Tennessee, there are some extremely important poultry indeed. If you arrive in the hotel lobby at 11.00 A.M. sharp, you will hear the elevator doors ping open and see some very unusual guests march out onto the awaiting red carpet.

Ducks have been swimming in the lobby fountain since the 1930s, when the hotel manager—in a moment of bourbon-inspired madness—decided that his live decoy ducks were the perfect decoration. The sight of ducks in the hotel's splendid marble fountain was an instant hit, and over 70 years later, the tradition continues.

At 5.00 P.M., these pampered poultry jump out of the fountain, shake themselves off, and waddle their way back into the elevator and up to a sumptuous rooftop penthouse, where their every duck whim is catered for by the hotel's Duckmaster.

Be gentle with the young.

JUVENAL (55–127AD)

Of course, the world's most famous duck will always be Walt Disney's Donald. Modeled on the pure white Pekin duck, Donald exemplifies all the arrogance and general quackery of a duck—the perfect foil to Mr. Nice Guy, Mickey Mouse. But, like any good duck, Donald didn't arrive alone; he brought with him an army of over 40 friends and family, from Pintail Duck, through Elvira Coot, Quackmore Duck, Lulubelle Loon, and Gladstone Gander, to his nephews Huey, Dewey, and Louie.

sitting duck

No matter how hard they try, no amount of preening,
posturing, and strutting can hide a duck's adorable comical
charm—whether it's a mallard drake gliding gracefully
across the pond, with his little feet paddling like mad just
beneath the water, or runner ducks like these dashing
around the barnyard like bowling pins on legs.

a duck to water

Ducks are found on every continent except
Antarctica. They quack in the foothills of the
Andes, waddle in the tropics of Africa, and
splash in the canals of Amsterdam. But
wherever they decide to set up home, you can
almost always be sure of one thing—water.

I saw a ship a-sailing,
A-sailing on the sea;
And, oh, it was all laden
With pretty things for thee!

... The captain was a duck,
With a packet on his back;
And when the ship began to move,
The captain said, "Quack! Quack!"

MOTHER GOOSE

off a duck's back

Not all ducks are water-lovers. The Australian wood
duck, for example, can barely swim and is much happier
observing goings-on from the branches of a nearby tree.
By contrast, North American bufflehead ducks are true
water babies—in fact, they even sleep on water!

It was very near flying, as when the duck rushes
through the water with an impulse of her wings,
throwing the spray about her before she can rise.

HENRY DAVID THOREAU,
A WEEK ON THE CONCORD AND MERRIMACK RIVERS, 1849

a battle of bills

The shape of a duck's bill will determine the way it feeds. Shoveler ducks have wide beaks, which they use to sift mud for insects and seeds. Sea ducks (who often don't look much like ducks at all) have long, narrow beaks with serrated edges—useful for snatching fish from the water.

Dabbling ducks, or puddle ducks, have short, broad beaks. When you see a duck assuming the ungraceful tail-up position in the pond, the chances are it is a puddle duck, stretching down in search of grasses and small insects for his lunch.

heading south

As the weather becomes harsh, the days shorter, and food scarce, ducks recognize the time to head for warmer waters to raise their young. They can fly thousands of miles, and the distinctive V-formation they use is a design of aerodynamic genius. By flying in each others' slipstream, the birds can conserve up to fifty percent of their energy. The stronger, more experienced birds will head the formation, changing leaders regularly to avoid exhaustion.

"When I find a thing,"
said the Duck:
"it's generally a frog,
or a worm."

LEWIS CARROLL, *ALICE'S
ADVENTURES IN WONDERLAND*, 1865

water babies

With the new season arrives the next generation of
ducklings. Often within hours of being born, the brood will
be led by their mother to the nearest water. This can be a
treacherous journey, sometimes involving a trek of several
miles crossing busy roads. But once they've arrived safely
at the watering hole, the important business of swimming
lessons can begin.

An adult duck's feathers will keep it snug and dry in the iciest of waters, thanks to a special oil-producing gland near the tail that provides a waterproof coating. A duckling's soft down doesn't have this waterproofing, and he can get very cold and wet if left to play in the water for too long. Luckily, a mother duck knows just how long the pool party should last.

God couldn't be everywhere, so he created mothers.

JEWISH PROVERB

I called the little pool a sea;
The little hills were big to me;
For I am very small.

ROBERT LOUIS STEVENSON, *MY KINGDOM* FROM
A CHILD'S GARDEN OF VERSES AND UNDERWOODS, 1913

acknowledgments

The publisher would like to thank Busbridge Lakes Waterfowl and Fran Young who kindly allowed us to photograph their wonderful ducks. Many thanks also to our model Georgia Smith.

Busbridge Lakes Waterfowl and Gardens
Hambledon Road
Godalming
Surrey GU8 4AY
United Kingdom
+ 44 (0)1483 421955
www.busbridgelakes.co.uk
Breeder of wildfowl and pheasants—over 100 species of birds, many endangered.
Pages 4–5, 6 left, 10–11, 18–23, 26–27, 32–35, 44–61

Useful websites:

The American Livestock Breeds Conservancy
www.albc-usa.org/waterfowl

Angel Wings Waterfowl rescue
www.waterfowlrescue.org

The Pet Duck and Goose Association
www.geocities.com/petduckassociation/